29.93

D1305676

JAN 2 2 2016

# D.I.Y. MAKE IT HAPPEN

# BASKETBALL TOURNAMENT

VIRGINIA LOH-HAGAN

354.6738

# ◉ 45th Parallel Press

Published in the United States of America by Cherry Lake Publishing
Ann Arbor, Michigan
www.cherrylakepublishing.com

Reading Adviser: Marla Conn, ReadAbility, Inc.
Book Designer: Felicia Macheske

Photo Credits: © glenda/Shutterstock.com, cover, 1, 15, 31; © nexus 7/Shutterstock.com, 3; © Blulz60/Shutterstock.com, 5; © Wisut Boonyasopit/Shutterstock.com, 7; © hxdbzxy/Shutterstock.com, 9; © Feng Yu/Shutterstock.com, 10, 31; © Jaimie Duplass/Shutterstock.com, 11; © Rommel Canlas/Shutterstock.com, 12; © Monkey Business Images/Shutterstock.com, 14, 18; © Torsak Thammachote/Shutterstock.com, 17; © aboikis/Shutterstock.com, 19; © Viacheslav Nikolaenko/Shutterstock.com, 20; © LHF Graphics/Shutterstock.com, 21; © Paul Velgos/Shutterstock.com, 22; © indigolotos/Shutterstock.com, 23; © Pressmaster/Shutterstock.com, 25; © Rawpixel/Shutterstock.com, 29; © www.BillionPhotos.com/Shutterstock.com, 30; © wavebreakmedia/Shutterstock.com, back cover; © Dora Zett/Shutterstock.com, back cover

Graphic Elements: © pashabo/Shutterstock.com, 6, back cover; © axako/Shutterstock.com, 7; © IreneArt/Shutterstock.com, 4, 8; © bokasin/Shutterstock.com, 11, 19; © Belausava Volha/Shutterstock.com, 12, 20; © Nik Merkulov/Shutterstock.com, 13; © Ya Tshey/Shutterstock.com, 16, 27; © kubais/Shutterstock.com, 16; © Sasha Nazim/v, 15, 24; © Ursa Major/Shutterstock.com, 23, 28; © Natalia Toropova/Shutterstock.com, 25, 27© Infomages/Shutterstock.com, 26, © topform/Shutterstock.com, back cover; © Art'nLera/Shutterstock.com, back cover

Copyright © 2016 by Cherry Lake Publishing
All rights reserved. No part of this book may be reproduced or utilized in any form or by any means without written permission from the publisher.

**45th Parallel Press** is an imprint of Cherry Lake Publishing.

Library of Congress Cataloging-in-Publication Data

Loh-Hagan, Virginia.
  Basketball tournament / by Virginia Loh-Hagan.
    pages cm. — (D.I.Y. Make it happen)
  ISBN 978-1-63470-495-3 (hardcover) — ISBN 978-1-63470-555-4 (pdf) — ISBN 978-1-63470-615-5 (paperback) — ISBN  978-1-63470-675-9 (ebook)
  1.  Basketball—Tournaments--Juvenile literature.  I. Title.
  GV885.1.L65 2016
  796.323'63—dc23
                                2015026840

Cherry Lake Publishing would like to acknowledge the work of The Partnership for 21st Century Skills.
Please visit *www.p21.org* for more information.

Printed in the United States of America
Corporate Graphics Inc.

## ABOUT THE AUTHOR

Dr. Virginia Loh-Hagan is an author, university professor, former classroom teacher, and curriculum designer. She was a member of the Holiday Bowl Committee. She volunteered at a basketball tournament. She lives in San Diego with her very tall husband and very naughty dogs. To learn more about her, visit www.virginialoh.com.

# TABLE OF CONTENTS

# CHAPTER ONE

# WHAT DOES IT MEAN TO START A BASKETBALL TOURNAMENT?

Do you love basketball? Do you love competing against others? Do you love planning things? Then starting a basketball tournament is the right project for you!

Basketball is a game. There are two teams. Each team has five players. Each team shoots a ball into a basket. That's how they score. They play on a court. A court is shaped like a rectangle. It has nets at both ends.

A basketball **tournament** is a series of games. Losing teams are kicked out.

Winning teams move on to the next level. Teams compete for a big prize. The winner is the champion.

Go to basketball tournaments.
Learn from others.

# KNOW THE LINGO

**Ball handler:** player with the ball

**Ball hog:** a player who does not pass the ball

**BEEF:** Balance, Eyes, Elbow, Follow-through (proper shooting form)

**Big dance:** another name for a tournament

**Dead ball:** when the ball is not in play

**Gunner:** a player who shoots the ball many times

**NBA:** National Basketball Association

**Pass:** throwing the ball to a teammate

**Rainbow:** a perfect high shot that looks like a rainbow

**Rebound:** getting the ball after a missed shot

**Shooter:** a player who takes a shot at the basket

**Swish**: a shot that goes in the net without hitting the rim

**Toilet bowl:** when the ball hits the rim on a certain angle and then circles around it

**Upset:** when a higher-ranked team loses to a lower-ranked team

**Weakside:** the side of the court away from the ball

**Zone defense:** when each player is responsible for defending a section of the court

Start a basketball tournament whenever you want. They're popular all year long.

Basketball players like tournaments. They like competing. They like playing. They like winning. They want to be the best.

People plan tournaments. They do it for different reasons. Some want to promote basketball. They want more people to play it. They want more people to know about it. Some want to raise money. Tournaments are great **fundraisers**. They make money. The money goes to a good cause.

Starting a basketball tournament is a good idea. You can meet new friends. You can exercise. You can make money for a charity.

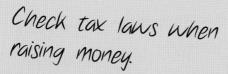

Check tax laws when raising money.

# CHAPTER TWO

# WHAT DO YOU NEED TO START A BASKETBALL TOURNAMENT?

Decide why you're hosting a tournament.

➡ Do you have a cause? Some tournaments raise money. They help buy gear for sports teams. Or support a charity.

➡ Identify your reason. Some people want to support basketball. Some people just want to play.

➡ Come up with a name for your event.

Decide on a place. You need a basketball court. You need seats.

➡ **Decide if you're playing indoors or outdoors.**

➡ **Consider places available to you. Examples are schools and parks.**

➡ **Figure out available dates. Host it over the weekend.**

➡ **Pick a good date. Check other events happening at the same time.**

➡ **Reserve the place. Do this way before the event.**

Consider hosting a tournament at the end of a sport season.

# Decide what type of tournament you want to host.

➡ **There's single elimination. Teams are kicked out when they lose. A team keeps playing as long as it wins. The winner is the undefeated team.**

➡ **There's double elimination. Each team can lose two times. Then it's kicked out.**

➡ **There's round-robin. Teams are divided into groups. They play everyone in their group. The team with the best record wins.**

➡ **There's 3-on-3. Teams have three players. They compete against each other. They play on one side of the court.**

---

# Decide the rules.

➡ **Decide who can play. Decide ages of players.**

➡ **Decide how players win.**

You can't have games without players.
Recruit teams.

➡ **Consider how many teams you need.**

➡ **Promote the event. Create posters. Hang them in public places. Tell everyone. Talk to friends. Talk to coaches.**

➡ **Create a Web site.**

➡ **Post registration information. People need to know how to sign up. Set a deadline.**

Decide rules for good sportsmanship.

# Get people to help you.

➡ Get **volunteers**. They give their time. They help. Ask friends. Ask family members.

➡ Get **referees**. They make decisions in a game.

➡ Get **scorekeepers**. They keep track of the points scored.

➡ You might want **sponsors**. Sponsors are businesses. They support your event. They pay for things. They pay for prizes. They get **exposure**. People see their names.

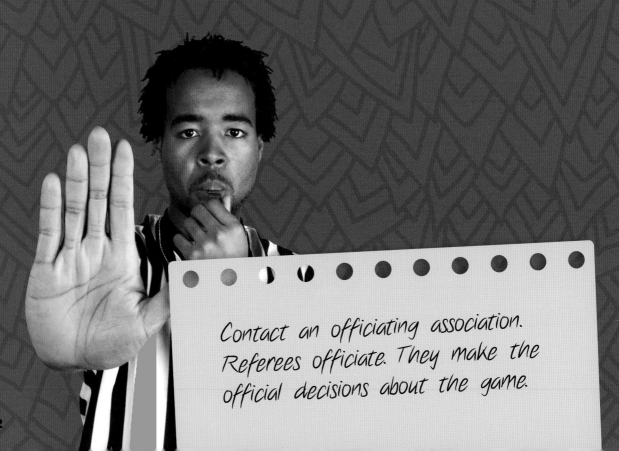

Contact an officiating association. Referees officiate. They make the official decisions about the game.

# TRY THIS!

Another way to make money is to host a raffle. A raffle is like a contest. People buy tickets. Each ticket gives them a chance of winning prizes. Make sure you have permission to host the raffle!

**You'll need:** tickets, prizes, cans for each prize, table

## Steps

1 Ask local businesses for prizes. Or ask people to give you prizes.

2 Place all the prizes on a table. Consider grouping small prizes together.

3 Place a can for raffle tickets in front of each prize.

4 Sell raffle tickets. Have people write their names on the tickets.

5 Have people put their raffle tickets in the cans. They choose the prizes they want.

6 At the end of the event, pick a name from each can. The name on the ticket wins the prize.

Get supplies. These are things you'll need for the tournament:

→ **Prizes. These can be medals or trophies. They're given to winners. A trophy is an object. It represents victory.**

→ **Basketballs. Make sure the balls have enough air.**

→ **Tables and chairs**

→ **Scoreboards. This is how scores are recorded. They're on a big board. This allows everyone to see.**

➡ **Score sheets.** Scorekeepers use these to track scores.

➡ **Whistles**

➡ **Speaker system.** This is so you can announce things.

➡ **Timers**

➡ **Water, snacks, and drinks**

➡ **First aid** kits. Players fall. They'll get hurt. First aid helps with cuts. It helps with scrapes.

*Make a list of everything you need.*

# CHAPTER THREE

# HOW DO YOU SET UP A BASKETBALL TOURNAMENT?

Create a tournament committee. A committee is a group of people who work on a project.

- The chair is the leader. This person makes the big decisions.

- The treasurer takes care of money. This person is in charge of registration.

- The publicity person lets the public know about the event. This person takes care of sponsors.

- The scheduling person takes care of the games.

- The facility manager takes care of the place.

- The greeter takes care of people. This person makes sure the coaches, players, and fans are having fun.

- The equipment manager takes care of the supplies.

## Advice from the Field
# KEVIN GREENTHAL

Kevin Greenthal is the president of the Muskego Warriors. The Warriors are from Wisconsin. They're a youth basketball team. They host a basketball tournament. It's for boys. It's for grades four through eight. He advises to focus on promoting. He said, "In order to attract teams, we used three main techniques. One, we posted the event on any Web site where basketball tournaments are posted. Two, we asked our coaches to reach out to other area coaches. Three, we contacted all teams that had participated in the past." He also advises being special. He said, "Think of ways that make your tournament unique. Differentiate yourself from other tournaments in the area. ... In addition to the raffle, we also held a 3-point contest, which the kids really enjoy. Not only did we raise funds for the program, but the kids and parents enjoyed the tournament."

Basketball tournaments are a fun way to meet people in your community.

Create a form for team entries. Each team has to turn in a form.

➡ **Ask for team name.**

➡ **Ask for players' names and ages.**

➡ **Ask for coach's name.**

➡ **Ask for contact information.**

Take care of registration. Make sure teams are signed up. They should sign up well before the event

→ Have each team pay a **fee**. A fee is a cost. Don't charge too much. The fee will cover your costs. Extra money can go to your cause.

→ Have each team wear matching shirts. This is how you'll tell teams apart.

→ Give teams copies of the rules.

→ Send teams a reminder about the tournament date.

---

Decide how you want to handle fans. You have choices.

→ Ask for **donations**. This is when people give you money.

→ Sell tickets. Have fans buy tickets to see the tournament.

Have teams sign waivers. This means you're not blamed for accidents.

Let teams know about the
schedule ahead of time.

# Set up the schedule.

➡ **Plan the day. Set times for the games. Set the time for announcing the winners.**

➡ **Allow time for a warm-up. Players need time before playing. They get ready.**

➡ **Provide time for time-outs. These are breaks. Players get hurt. Players need water. Players need to think. They take breaks for these things.**

---

# Set up brackets. The brackets show the teams for each game. They show the winners of each game.

➡ **Set up the first teams to play.**

➡ **Match teams randomly. This means in no order. You can pick the teams out of a hat.**

➡ **After each game, update the brackets.**

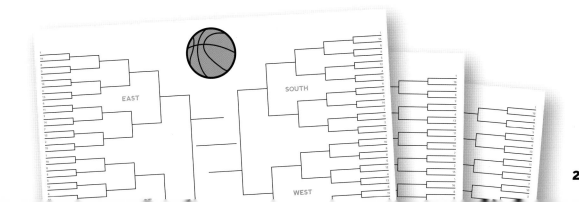

Sell drinks and snacks. People get hungry. People get thirsty. You can make more money.

➡ **Buy drinks. Get water. Get soda. Get fruit juice.**

➡ **Buy snacks. Get candy. Get popcorn. Get nuts. Get chips. Get cookies.**

➡ **Assign someone to take care of the money. This person will also watch the food and drinks.**

There are other ways to make money. People will buy things to remember the event.

➡ **Sell shirts. The shirts should have the date. They should have the tournament name.**

➡ **Create programs. Sell them. Include the schedule. Include the players' names. Include their pictures. Include some fun facts. Ask for this information on the entry form.**

T-shirts are a fun way to remember the tournament.

# CHAPTER FOUR

# HOW DO YOU RUN A BASKETBALL TOURNAMENT?

You've got players. You've got basketball courts. You're ready to host the tournament! There are things to do before the tournament.

➡ Set up the court. Make sure it's ready for the games.

➡ Set up a supply center.

➡ Set up where you want the players and referees.

➡ Set up where you want the scorekeepers.

➡ Set up the scoreboards.

- Set up the snacks and drinks area. Make sure you protect the money.

- Set up the seats for fans.

- Greet people. Say hello to the players, coaches, and fans.

- Set up the brackets for the first games.

- Introduce the tournament.

Assign volunteers to help you set up. Draw a map of how you want things.

# QUICK TIPS

- Rent tables to other people. Let them sell things. They're called vendors.

- Ask a local celebrity to come. A celebrity is a famous person. The celebrity can play. Or announce things. Or give the trophy.

- Invite the local newspaper to send a reporter. The reporter might take pictures. The reporter might write a news story. This promotes future events.

- Consider the fans' experience. You want fans to have fun. You want them to bring people. Make sure you provide enough activities for them.

- Invite rival teams. Rivals are like enemies. They compete against each other.

- Ask the school band to perform. This means more people will be at your tournament. Create an area for them.

- Get some cheerleaders. They pep up the fans.

- Put garbage cans everywhere.

- Clean team benches. Do this after every game.

The tournament will be busy. There will be lots of things happening. It'll be noisy. It'll be high energy. There are things to do during the tournament.

⇒ **Walk around. Check things.**

⇒ **Make sure helpers are where they should be.**

⇒ **Make sure everyone has what he or she needs.**

⇒ **Make sure there are enough supplies.**

⇒ **Keep track of the scores. Keep track of the winners. Update the brackets. Update the scoreboards.**

⇒ **Take pictures. Pictures promote your event. Post them online.**

⇒ **Solve problems. People may be upset about losing. People may get mad. Work with them. Calm them down.**

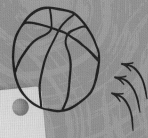

*Make a list of things you need to check on.*

There are things to do after the tournament.

➡ Announce the winning team. Announce the teams that came in second and third. Give out trophies or medals.

➡ Thank everyone for coming.

➡ Thank the players. Thank the coaches.

➡ Thank your helpers.

➡ If you're hosting another event, ask people to come again.

➡ Clean up. Don't leave a mess. You might want to use the place again.

➡ Send a note to the players. Thank them again. Ask them to give you feedback. Have them tell you what they liked. Have them tell you what you can improve.

Starting a basketball tournament is a lot of work. But it's also a lot of fun!

Have an awards ceremony. Invite winners and their families. Give different awards. Give awards for best player, most improved, and others.

# D.I.Y. EXAMPLE!

| STEPS | EXAMPLES |
| --- | --- |
| **Purpose** | To raise funds for the neighborhood basketball team's uniforms and bus trips |
| **Name** | The First Annual B-Ball Tournament |
| **Place** | School gym |
| **Type** | Single elimination |
| **Rules** | <ul><li>Students in grades four through six can play.</li><li>Both boys and girls can play.</li><li>Teams are kicked out when they lose.</li><li>Winner is the undefeated team.</li></ul> |

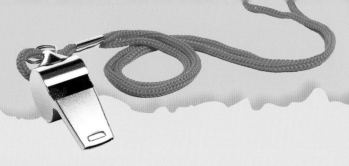

| STEPS | EXAMPLES |
|---|---|
| **Fees** | <ul><li>Team entry fee: $15</li><li>Fan fee: $3</li><li>Program: $5</li><li>Snacks: $2</li><li>Drinks: $1</li></ul> |
| **Promotion and marketing plan** | <ul><li>Send an e-mail to the parent-teacher organization members.</li><li>Create posters. Put them all over the school.</li><li>Get sponsors for sections of the gym: seats, court, scorekeeper area, snacks and drinks area. Place their names in that area.</li><li>Sell advertising space in the program.</li></ul> |

# GLOSSARY

**brackets** (BRAK-its) diagrams of tournament players showing who's playing and the winners

**committee** (kuh-MIT-ee) a group of people who work on a project

**donations** (doh-NAY-shuhnz) money gifts

**double elimination** (DUHB-uhl ih-lim-uh-NAY-shun) a type of tournament in which each team can lose two times before being kicked out

**exposure** (ik-SPOH-zhur) letting people know who you are

**facility** (fuh-SIL-ih-tee) place

**fee** (FEE) cost

**first aid** (FURST AYD) help for cuts and scrapes; help given to people who hurt themselves before medical help can be provided

**fundraisers** (FUHND-rayz-urz) events that raise money for a good cause

**publicity** (puh-BLIS-ih-tee) promotion and marketing

**randomly** (RAN-duhm-lee) done in no order

**referees** (ref-uh-REEZ) officials; they make decisions about the game.

**registration** (rej-ih-STRAY-shuhn) the process of signing up

**scoreboards** (SKOR-bordz) big boards that have scores on them

**scorekeepers** (SKOR-kee-purz) people who keep scores

**single elimination** (SING-uhl ih-lim-uh-NAY-shun) type of tournament in which teams are kicked out when they lose and winning teams keep playing

**sponsors** (SPAHN-surz) businesses or people who support events by paying for things for exposure

**tournament** (TOOR-nuh-muhnt) series of games or contests

**treasurer** (TREZH-ur-ur) person who takes care of money

**trophies** (TROH-feez) prizes that are given to winners

**volunteers** (vah-luhn-TEERZ) helpers who don't get paid

# INDEX

# LEARN MORE

## BOOKS

Bekkering, Annalise. *NCAA Basketball*. New York: AV2 by Weigl, 2014.

Silverman, Drew. *The NBA Finals*. Minneapolis: ABDO Publishing, 2013.

## WEB SITES

Amateur Athletic Union: www.aausports.org

How Stuff Works—"How to Organize a Basketball Tournament": http://lifestyle.howstuffworks.com/event-planning/how-to-host/how-to-organize-basketball-tournament.htm

United States Basketball Association: www.usbahoops.com